I CAN DO IT · 1

PRINTING

Written and illustrated by
HOWARD MELL & ERIC FISHER

SCHOFIELD & SIMS LTD · HUDDERSFIELD

7217 4500 8

Reprinted September 1968

Printed in Great Britain by
W. S. Cowell Ltd at the Butter Market, Ipswich

Introduction to the series

The "I Can Do It" series is an attempt to solve some of the problems presented to non-specialist teachers of art and craft activities in the Primary school.

In the course of years of experience in training teachers and in meeting serving teachers both in school and on courses in art and craft, we have found that a high proportion of teachers are, for a variety of reasons, chary of the subject or are letting their children miss much of the variety, enjoyment and even excitement which this part of creative activities can bring.

A very large number of teachers are anxious to know how to extend work in art and craft but generally lack confidence in their abilities. We must, therefore, emphasise that if you do not feel confident in your own technical ability, the first requirement is not *expertise* but *enthusiasm*. If you are interested and can create interest, then the first obstacle is overcome. Many schools have a rich experience in art and craft to offer to children not because their staffs are specialist art teachers but because they provide the right atmosphere and the necessary interest.

There are books available on the philosophy of the subject and a number, which are very sound, dealing with the characteristics and development of children's art and with programmes of activities and so on. Our experience is that teachers also want something which explains *how to do it*. We have attempted to meet this need by aiming the series at the child and by giving additional notes in the teacher's books. These you will find interleaved so that you are always at or very near the activity in question. You will find comments on points to watch, addresses for sources of materials, suggestions on alternatives, titles of recommended books etc.

These books should make it plain that we believe that finding out about the potentialities and limitations of materials is in itself a strong motivation to rich creative work and to children's learning. But it must be emphasised that these are not the only forms of stimulation. The environment, stories, visits, natural and "found" objects, animals, things seen under a magnifying glass . . . . these are a few of the many things which can be used by the teacher to increase the value of this series and to help so much in the child's general education. We urge you not to rely on the books as a series of "tips". Plenty of detail on procedure is given, but the child is constantly urged to try variations, to make additions, to see what happens if . . . . The authors make no claim to know all the answers. If pupils appear to be tackling a problem in a way quite different from that suggested in the books, they should be encouraged to do so unless it is evident that imminent disaster and frustration can be the only result. Their way may be better than ours.

The books cannot and are not intended to replace the teacher. They provide sufficient guidance and direction to ensure success and yet leave tremendous scope for personal exploration and experiment — each section contains a basic idea from which the child (and the teacher) can depart as is thought fit. Their purpose is to make the child's activity richer and more purposeful; to guide, help, give confidence and so sustain the child's involvement longer than might otherwise have been the case.

As ever, the teacher is the key for the provision of motivation and stimulation, for setting the climate in which creative activities can flourish and in which children can grow and develop. Use the books, therefore, in any way you please, adapting, amending, choosing whatever activity suits your programme of work. If, by using them, the books help to encourage the children to use all their senses, to be more aware and perceptive, then they will not have been written in vain.

Contents

A word of advice

You will find that you can enjoy making the things in this book much more if you remember some simple rules:

Before you begin: always cover your desk with newspaper. Put out the things you need.

When you are working: do not let things get too messy.

When you have finished: clean the things you have used and put them away. Put scraps in the wastepaper basket.

Keep things tidy – including yourself!

Preface to printing

A variety of printing methods is presented for the child to tackle. Most of them are capable of development and we urge that the pupil be encouraged to add to what has already been printed to see whether they improve the work. Above all, *techniques can be mixed* and the resulting work made more attractive — cf. sponge and potato, prints with brush marks and so on.

If at all possible, plenty of interesting printed material should be on show and made the subject of discussion. Pieces of printed fabric, wallpaper etc., illustrating ways in which the printing process is used, provide stimulation and show the child that his work is not only pleasurable and a means of creating visual effects but is linked with everyday life.

The book, here and there, suggests that the child, in making articles, can use what he has printed. Similarly, some of the activities can be used for decorating articles already made, e.g. table mats, aprons, bags, books etc. It is hoped that the teacher can add more ideas in this area as it gives additional purpose to the printing activities.

The addresses for materials and the titles of recommended books are collated at the end of the notes to give a convenient point of reference.

The authors wish to acknowledge the kind co-operation of Miss P. M. Roper and Mrs. G. Coupland.

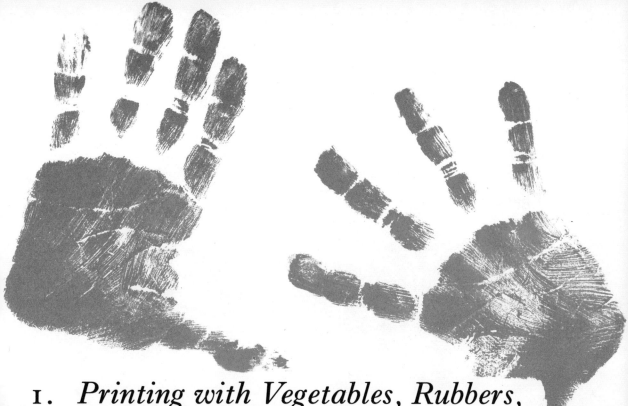

1. *Printing with Vegetables, Rubbers, Leaves and other things*

Have you ever made dirty marks on the floor with your shoes? "Oh, what a mess!" says mother. Or perhaps she is looking at the towel when you haven't *really* washed your hands before drying them.

We can see some of these marks here. They are called PRINTS. What sort of prints do detectives look for? What other prints can you think of?

You can make a lot of prints. Have you an india-rubber (the rubber you rub out pencil and other marks with)? You can make prints with it.

Mix some thick paint. Brush it on to one side of the rubber. Press the side you have painted on to a piece of paper. Try this again. You are *printing*. Here are some prints I have made.

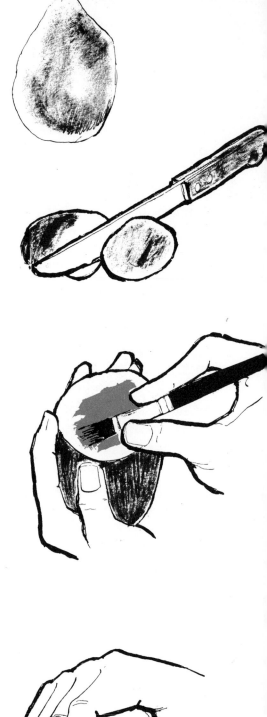

Beg a potato from your mother, or perhaps your teacher has one for you. Cut it in two like the potato in the picture. Your teacher may wish to cut it for you.

Mix some *thick* paint. Brush it on that flat side of the potato. Press the potato down hard on to your paper. Try not to move the potato. What happens if you do? Lift the potato up.

You have made a potato print. Now print some more.

Before starting other forms of printing, an interesting session taking fingerprints, similar to the police method, could take place. Another useful activity, if you are able to get the raw materials, is the taking of spoor prints. Place the head of a toad-stool, gills down on a piece of paper (the results are more easily seen on tinted paper). Cover with a bowl or basin for a few days. A print should appear.

This section goes somewhat further than the potato printing generally found in schools. A very large number of variations is possible which can lead to a much richer experience and to highly interesting results.

The most common error which pupils make is to mix too much water with the paint. Thin paint, of course, can give results of a certain quality, but generally the paint is best when it is rather stiff and tacky.

A small chapter could be written on the technique of cutting the potato and printing with it. A few useful points are given here:

Use a large knife with a wide blade such as a large kitchen knife or butcher's knife to cut the potato into pieces. Hold the potato firmly on the desk. A sawing action is sometimes preferred by some teachers. The object is to get a *flat* surface which will print evenly. A small knife is likely to leave ridges.

Some potatoes produce a great deal of moisture when cut. It helps the printing process to dry the potato with a rag or paper towel before applying the paint.

The channels dug out of the potato can be quite shallow though pupils will find from experience what the limits are. The type of paper and the consistency of the paint will have a bearing on this.

Some pupils, when urged to cut away the potato, produce a miniature mountain range or opencast working. This can be interesting carving but does not produce attractive printing results. Let them find out what happens, but be ready with your help if the pupil is disappointed.

A pocket knife, lino tool, or even a pen nib reversed in its holder can give good results.

Whilst most papers are usable a slightly absorbent paper is fine. A thin, non-glossy paper is cheap and newspaper itself is more than acceptable.

Several layers of newspaper on the table or desk top will make a slightly resilient printing surface aiding the production of good prints as well as tidiness and clearing up into the bargain. To get a good, even print, hold the potato steady but change pressure alternately from thumb to finger side — a rock and roll *pressure* rather than *movement*.

These are some patterns. They were printed with a potato. What happens if you dig out some of the potato before you print with it? A penholder or a knife will be good for digging out. Does the print look better? Try making more prints.
Is your paint thick enough? Your prints will be better if the paint is not thin.

Cut out some more potato. Print it. How much better can you make it? Can you do better starting with a fresh piece of potato? Try and see.

Here are some prints made in this way. But the *shape* of the potato is different. How does it differ from yours? *You* can make this shape. The drawing shows you how. Is it too difficult? If it is, ask your teacher to help you.

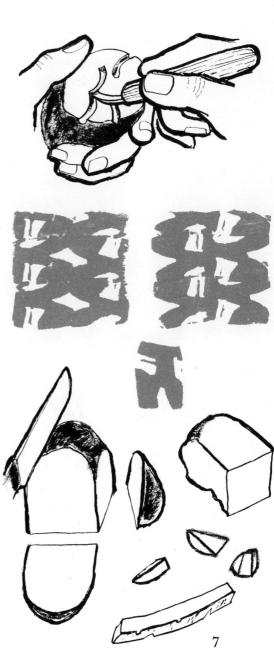

Now cut out some of the side you are going to print.

Put on the paint and print. If you print the same piece several times you can cover the whole of your paper. Have you some more paper? Try making different patterns. How many can you make? Are you trying different colours and different shapes?

Why not use some of the little pieces of potato you have cut off? Try printing some of these on a piece of paper. Try printing some on top of the prints you made with the big pieces. Does this make the pattern better?

Would the prints look better if you used different colours? See what happens when you try one colour printed on top of another. Do you like it?

Do you think you can print with a carrot? Can you use a piece of turnip? Try them.

After a preliminary stamping about on the printing paper, some guidance on spacing, rhythm, etc. may be needed. The potato can be "walked" across the paper in a kind of waddle movement, or successive prints can be made to touch one another.

All kinds of interlocking patterns can be produced by older juniors and some younger ones in response to this suggestion:

Cut a groove from the potato which enters at one side and leaves at another. How many ways can you print the potato so that the spaces join up?

The sketch shows the idea. Having done this, another piece can then be taken out of the potato and the resultant combinations of prints compared and considered.

One printing method which can be worked by individuals, but which is also useful for a group activity, is to start in the middle and, using small pieces of potato, work outwards radially. You will readily think of variants, but do remember that small pieces of the potato, including the trimmings, can be used for pattern and picture making (cf. the bird on page 13). Carrots, turnips, swedes all give pleasing granular printed textures when the paint is applied in certain consistencies. Why keep to the potato when you can so easily give variety?

The strip of turnip or swede is an especially enjoyable exercise. Held in both hands, it can be waddled across the paper, or one hand can be held firm and the other skidded. It can be bent or stretched; the full thickness or only the edge used. The children themselves will think of other ways. Over-enthusiasm may break the strip, but a replacement is easy and cheap. Patterns based on these curved marks are produced, but highly interesting and often amusing birds, animals etc., can emerge.

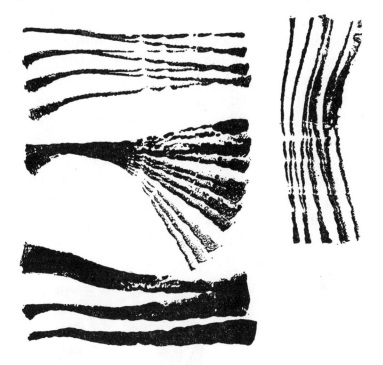

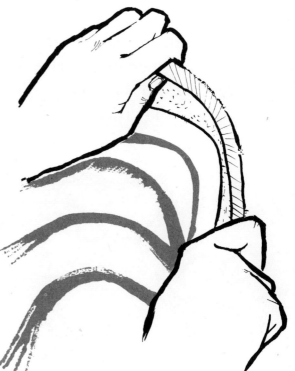

Here is a strip of turnip. It is long but not very thick. Cut a piece like this for yourself. Or perhaps your teacher has cut one for you. Put some thick paint on one of the long sides.

Hold an end of the strip in each hand. Can you bend the strip? Be careful! If you bend it too much, the turnip soon breaks. Try printing the strip when it is bent.

Put on more paint. Bend the strip. Print again. Try different bends. Try other colours.

Which prints are best? Can you make better patterns by making the prints cross one another?

Some of the turnip prints in the picture have had potato prints added. Which are they? Can *you* use potato and turnip in the same pattern?

What other things can you use for printing?

Here are some. Try them! Do you like the prints they make? Can you print one on top of the other?

What other things are you going to try? Do they print well? Can they be used with some of the things you have already tried?

A joiner will give you some small pieces of wood. Ask him for some *flat* pieces. Now fix something on one of the pieces with glue. The drawings show some of the things I have tried.

What have *you* got that you can try? When you have glued something on the piece of wood, brush on some thick paint. Press hard down on your paper. Lift off. What happens?

Make a lot more prints. See if you can fill your piece of paper. What happens when you print one thing on top of another? Did you use a different colour? Why?

Here, and in the three following pages, the child is asked to investigate the possibilities of mark-making objects. You can help by having odds and ends available but children will bring lots of things to try.

Wood is the best material on which to affix string, rubber and so on, but empty tobacco tins and other firm boxes will do. Try them out! Bostik, Seccotine or rubber solution will hold the materials on the block.

Efforts should be made all the time, by discussion and display, to draw the pupils' attention to the qualities of the marks they are making — speckled, granular, etc. — and the rich gradations of tone and colour which they will achieve.

Children are often reluctant to add to a pattern for fear of "spoiling" it, but the great advantage of printing as a creative activity is that an effect can be repeated many times. One way of keeping some of the printing "unspoiled" is to encourage the pupil to add marks and/or overprint just a section of the work, so that both the first pattern and the later work can be seen and compared.

Do encourage the adding of further marks. A simple second shape overprinted on the first in a different colour can add a lot of interest to the pattern and children will experience greater satisfaction.

Some teachers seem to think that adding brush marks to printed work is a form of cheating! We do not suggest that such marks should always be added—far from it—but these additions can make the pattern more interesting and it is all part of the finding out process.

I printed this pattern. First I printed a piece of sponge. I put each print against another so that I covered all my paper. Then I used a piece of wood with string glued to it. I printed the string on top of the sponge prints. I used one colour for the sponge and another colour for the string.

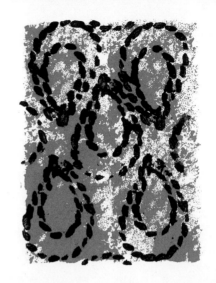

What things are you printing? Are you trying one print on top of others? Which colours do you like best together?

If you print one colour on top of another, is there any difference if you wait for the first colour to dry? Perhaps you like the pattern better? Or do you like both ways?

Can you make your prints look better? Try adding some other marks – brush marks or crayon marks. What other marks can you add? Discuss this with your teacher.

Do you like to experiment? Why not try a lot of different things that make marks? You may find some exciting things to print with. They could make very interesting patterns.

The pictures here show some of the things I have tried. The first one is a piece of wood with drawing pins pushed into the side. Then string is wrapped round the wood in different ways. The drawing pins stop the string from slipping. If some paint or ink is put on the string you can print it. Cover the string with thin paper. Rub the paper with your fingers to get a print. You can use the piece of wood over and over again. To change the pattern, take off the string and wrap it on again in a different way.

What are the other things in the drawings? Are *you* going to try printing some of them?

You can use one of your hands to make prints and patterns. What other things will you try?

These are further attempts to get the child to try things out. The string-on-wood patterns have a distinct character which older children will be quick to appreciate. Their linear quality, when repeated and joined up can produce an overall effect quite different from, say, the sponge print. It is one more illustration of what can happen if one encourages the trying out of new ideas.

The drawings on the page opposite show a few items which the children could try. They are put there only as a beginning, to get things moving. A list of objects is really not needed; try anything!

A variant, worth trying with the flatter objects, is to place *thin* paper over the object and then to roll on the colour. The point of the object then appears as a darker area than the surrounding colour.

Potato-print pictures have a charm all their own which derives from the rhythm of the repeated shape and from the granular texture of the print. These produce subtle variations of colour quite unlike those possible with a brush.

Reference is made to the process of printing with cardboard. Again, many articles can produce useful results and excellent pictures can be produced using pieces of embossed wallpaper, leather (cf. alligator leather), hardboard (the textured side), lace, doyleys and so on, all coated with colour and pressed on the paper. Consider this in connection with pages 20 to 28.

A basic paper or card shape — or a painted shape — can be decorated with printed shapes.

Did you know that you can make *pictures* as well as patterns
by printing?
Look at the picture here! It is a bird. What sort of bird is it?
It was made by printing with different pieces of potato.
Try making some pictures yourself.
Think of all the many things you can make pictures of:
birds, animals, people.
I am sure you can think of many more.
Discuss this with your teacher.
There are some more pictures on page 27.
Some of these are printed by using cardboard.
We will try this later.

Making a printing pad

With a printing pad, you can print faster. Using a brush is much slower. Several people can use the same printing pad.

Find some tin lids – really big ones. I use lids from big boxes of powder paint. Now you need some pieces of rag. Flannel is good, or you can use several layers of thinner cloth.

Another very useful material is thin sponge sheeting. Perhaps your teacher has some. The kind called foam sponge is good and cheap.
Cut any of these to fit the lid.
Mix some paint and put just enough into the lid to cover the bottom.

Then put in the material you have cut. What happens in a few minutes? Press your potato (or whatever you are printing with) on to the pad.

A temporary printing pad can be made from several (12 to 30) sheets of newsprint placed in a box lid and soaked with powder colour.

Some teachers have told us that the pad described opposite does not allow rich colour effects. We have convinced them that this is not so, by showing that the paint consistency is the controlling factor. Do not get it too thin unless a pale colour is required. If the pad is too soggy and wet, then wet and messy prints will result.

Encourage a "press and print" system; that is, take *one* print from *one* pressing then press on the pad again. More even colouring will result.

Sponge sheeting will dry hard. Dipping it in water will restore its softness.

A brush can be used in place of the pad; it allows the use of paint which is much thicker than is possible with a pad. One is not necessarily better than the other however, and, of course, both can be used effectively together.

Have you got enough colour from the pad? If not, put more colour in the lid.

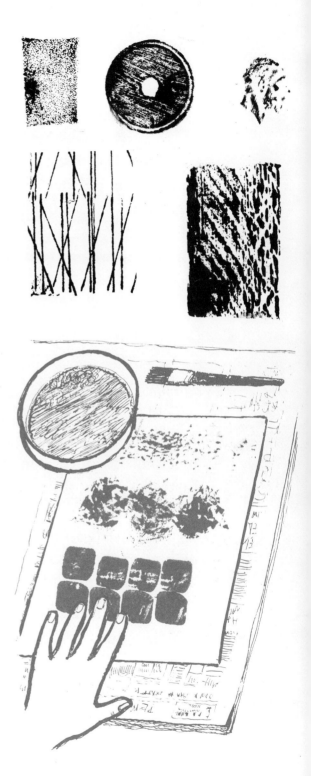

Try again. Press on the pad and then print on the paper. Is your print clear? Is the colour as deep as you want it? When it is deep enough, go on and print some more.

Try pressing different things on the pad and printing them. Which make good prints? Which make poor prints? Is the print as good as when you use a brush for putting on the colour?

Now choose which way you like.

Sometimes I use a brush and sometimes I use a pad. Sometimes I use both. Can you think why?

Using a roller to print with

Later, you can read about many
ways of using a roller. Some of the
things you have already printed
with can have the colour put on to
them with a roller. Here is the way
to do it.

You will need :
  A rubber roller.
  A sheet of metal or glass. (A
  piece of formica can be used
  instead.) A useful size is 10 in. by
  8 in.
  Temperapaste or similar colour,
  or lino or duplicating ink.
  Thin paper and old newspapers.

Put some sheets of newspaper on
the desk. Lay the metal, formica or
glass sheet on top.

Rubber rollers are a very handy item of equipment for the classroom and they will last for many years given care in cleaning them after use. Substitutes for a roller are possible, e.g. the plastic bottles which have contained washing-up liquid. Some splendid, though rather expensive, transparent plastic rollers are produced by T. N. Lawrence & Son, 2–4 Bleeding Heart Yard, Greville St., Hatton Garden, London E.C.1.

A recipe for using Vaseline is given on page 43.

Water-based lino inks are excellent and are obtainable from most suppliers. Margros and Reeves, among others, sell large tubes which save money. The colour can be cleaned off with water and this is particularly important when it is necessary to get the colour off the child!

A little practice will soon reveal the possibilities of this method of printing.

In the suggestions on this page, the leaf etc. acts as a mask which leaves its shape uncoloured on the paper when removed. This can be used as an introduction to talking about *positive* and *negative* shapes.

Newspaper is most acceptable for printing on, the letter-press giving its own texture.

Put a few blobs of ink or colour on the sheet. Now spread the colour around on the sheet by moving the roller backwards and forwards until the roller is covered with colour.

Choose what you want to print. It could be a leaf or a feather or some grasses. Or have you some other thing you want to try?

Lay it down flat on a piece of paper – a piece of newspaper will do. Run the roller all over it until the paper is covered with colour. If you need more colour, run the roller over the sheet of glass or metal again.

When the paper is covered, lift off the object you have printed. What has happened on the paper? The picture here shows a plant some children printed. Can you say what sort of plant it is?

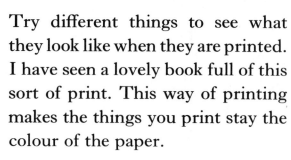

Try different things to see what they look like when they are printed. I have seen a lovely book full of this sort of print. This way of printing makes the things you print stay the colour of the paper.

Now, here is how to colour the thing you print: Put a piece of newspaper or any old paper on the desk. Have you covered the desk with other newspaper first?

Lay what you are going to print on the piece of paper. Run the roller over it until what you are printing is covered with colour.

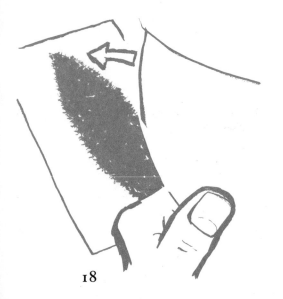

Put another piece of paper on the desk. Lift up the leaf, or what it is you are printing, and put it coloured side down on this new piece of paper. Try not to get your fingers *too* dirty! Cover what you are printing with another piece of paper.

Hold the paper with one hand and rub it all over with the other. Be sure to rub hard all over what you are printing. If you like, you can use the back of a spoon to rub with.

Lift off the top paper and then the thing you are printing. You should have a good, clear print to look at. You can see some leaf prints I have done on this page.

Can you make more of these prints? What other things can you print in this way?

Many of the printing ideas in this book work very well with a roller.

On page 43 you can read how to make prints using vaseline mixed with paint. The mixture is used with a roller. Leaves and plants and other things covered with the vaseline mixture make very good prints.

2. *Printing with Cardboard, Stencils and Paper Shapes*

Cardboard prints

You will need :
    Scrap card. (Old box lids, Christ-
mas or birthday cards. Old post
cards are very good.) Paint and
brush or roller and colour.
    Scissors. Thin paper. Glue.

Cut a piece of card like the one in
the picture. Not *too* big!

What is this shape called?

Now cut some other, smaller shapes.
Make the shapes as interesting as
you can.

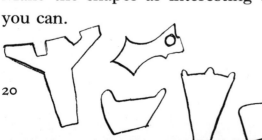

The prints at the top of page 20 give an idea of what can happen when printing from cardboard shapes — the print is not always even. The results can be affected by several factors: the quality of the card (a smooth faced card does not usually soak up too much colour); the thickness of the paint and how many times the card has been charged with colour. Usually, the card prints better when it has taken up some of the colour after being used several times.

When this method is used, the colour will sometimes be put inadvertently on the background as well as on the shapes themselves. If the colour is kept stiff or tacky, there is not as much difficulty keeping it to the raised areas as one might expect. Control is easier if the colour is applied with a roller or is dabbed on. Very often the "unwanted" colour can add to the attractiveness of the print.

Another way of using cardboard shapes is shown on page 23.

Stick them on to the first shape you cut. Now brush some thick colour on to the shapes you have glued, or *roll* some colour on them. Make sure the colour goes only on to the glued shapes.

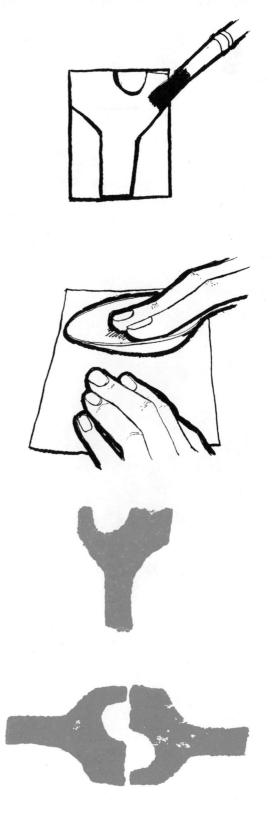

Put a piece of thin paper on top. Press it against the card with your fingers. Rub the paper hard where it covers the shapes. Better still, rub with the back of a spoon or a ruler or a piece of wood. Be sure to rub the paper hard.

Take off the paper. Have you got a good print? Try again if you are disappointed.

Try different colours. See if you can make your pattern more interesting. Start again – cut some different shapes. Which shapes do you like best?

Turn your paper round so that the top is at the bottom. Put a different

colour on the cardboard. Print the paper again. Do you like the pattern? Can you make it better? Why not see what happens by printing different shapes on top of one another? You can do it if you have two pieces of card each with shapes glued on.

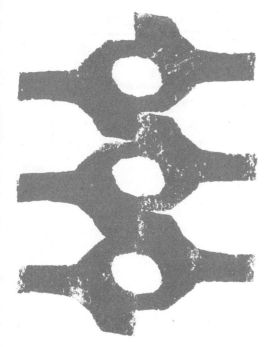

Try printing other things on top of the cardboard prints. Does this make the prints look better?

What does the print look like if you first cover the paper with potato or sponge or other shapes and then print cardboard shapes on top?

Can you get interesting prints by sticking other things to the piece of cardboard?

The picture shows a pattern printed from beans glued to cardboard. What other sorts of prints can you make, using other things glued to the card?

Printing edge to edge, face to face, upside down, turning each successive stamp through 90° — these are some of the elements of pattern making. These changes help to make the operation enjoyable and instructive, with a growing realisation that the spaces left contribute as much to the design as the stamped, coloured areas; see the Teachers Notes and illustration for page 8.

Peas, lentils, buttons, anything giving shallow relief, are suitable for attachment to a cardboard base.

More cardboard prints

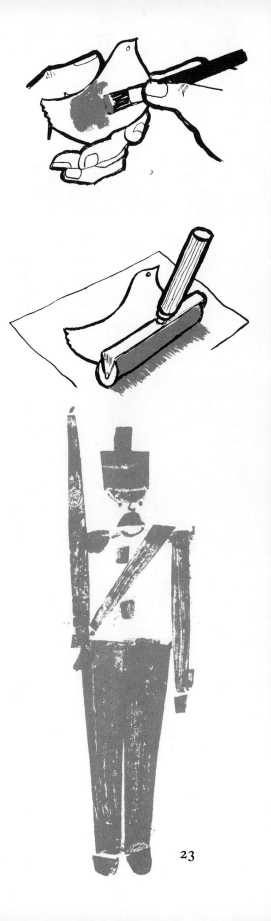

You will need :
  The same things as before, but
  no glue.

Put newspaper on the desk. Put your
paper down flat on the newspaper.

Cut some shapes out of the card.
Put them on the newspaper. Use a
brush or roller and colour the
shapes one at a time. Lift up each
shape and press it on to the paper.

Press hard. Decide how many times
you are going to print each shape
to make the pattern as clear as you
can. Look at the pattern and then
choose the shapes you can add to
make it even better.

Do you like it best made up of
different shapes, or with one shape
printed in two or three colours?
Perhaps you prefer several shapes
with two or three colours. I printed
the soldier with one or two different
pieces of card.

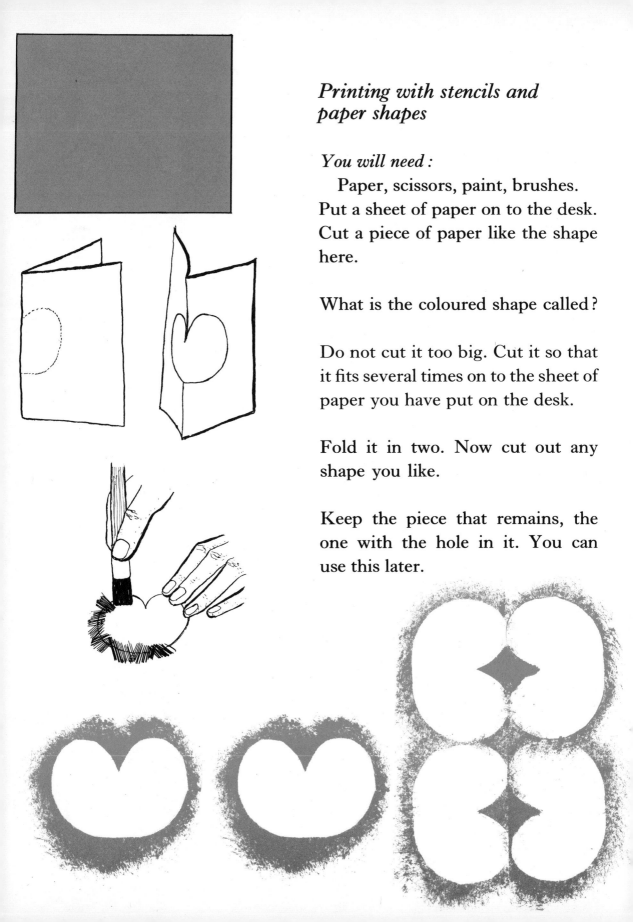

Printing with stencils and paper shapes

You will need :

Paper, scissors, paint, brushes.
Put a sheet of paper on to the desk.
Cut a piece of paper like the shape
here.

What is the coloured shape called?

Do not cut it too big. Cut it so that
it fits several times on to the sheet of
paper you have put on the desk.

Fold it in two. Now cut out any
shape you like.

Keep the piece that remains, the
one with the hole in it. You can
use this later.

A brush with short, stiff bristles is best for stencils. Most suppliers sell special stencil brushes but there is no real need to spend money on them. An old toothbrush is useful and an old shaving brush or paint brushes with their bristles cut are fine. Incidentally, they make interesting textures when dabbed on independently of cut shapes.

The main precaution is to ensure that the colour does not run under the edge of the stencil. Hold the stencil firmly down at the edges. One idea is to drag the brush *inwards* when using the stencil and *outwards* when using the shape.

Keep the paint thick to avoid runs etc.

Put the shape you have cut on to the
sheet of paper. Press down the
edges of the shape with the fingers
of one hand.

Paint all round the shape. Keep the
paint fairly thick and drag the brush
across the edge of the shape outwards on to the paper.

Can you see why you must hold
down the edges of the shape?

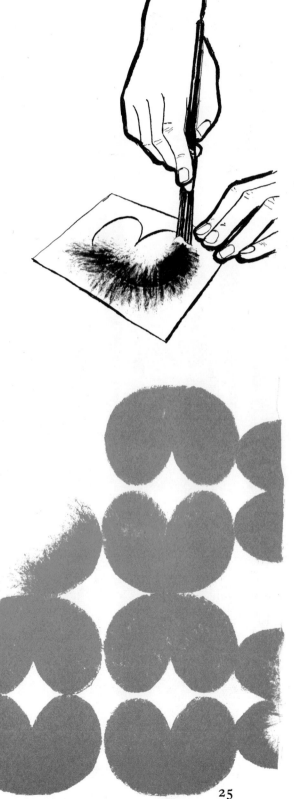

When you have painted all round
the shape, lift it off the paper. Move
it to another part of the paper and
paint round it again.

Cover your paper with coloured
shapes. The pictures opposite show
you how.

What can you add to make the pattern better?

Another shape? Another colour? Or have you a special idea of your own?

You can use the piece of paper with the hole in it. It is called a *stencil*.

Hold it flat on your piece of paper. Fill the space with paint. Look at the pictures on page 25. Remember to keep the paint fairly thick. Paint more shapes. How are you going to fill the paper?

There are many ways of using shapes and stencils for making very good patterns. Try different shapes and add different prints. You will soon make better patterns. Ask yourself which is the pattern you like best. Discuss your work with your teacher.

I have printed some shapes here with a stencil. Then I added more marks with potato. The small prints were added with a cork!

But *must* you start with a shape or a stencil? Of course not! You can start with other prints and *then* add the shapes or the stencil prints.

Another way is to start with one big shape and then print on top. The owl here was made from pieces of tissue paper. Potato prints were put on top.

I am sure you can think of all sorts of ways of beginning to print and all sorts of things to print together. Somebody is going to say "Now isn't that interesting!"

Making pictures with card and paper

Try making pictures with different shapes cut from cardboard and paper. If you want to, you can print some or all of your shapes several times. There is a picture made like this here. Can you see how it was done? The houses are the same shape in this picture but they were printed in different colours.

The lions were made from one cardboard shape and the trees from two shapes. Just think of all the different pictures you can make with shapes. Try using shapes and then adding other things with a brush and colour, or other articles you can print with. The boat was cut from a piece of old wallpaper and the portholes were printed with a round stick. The sea is printed with a potato and . . . what else?

YOU try your own ideas. What are you going to start with? What other things are you going to use?

On page 27, the owl again shows the point we constantly reiterate: that techniques can be mixed. The owl began life as a series of torn up pieces of tissue paper. Overprinting added interest and colour. Encourage the use of different types of printing on one pattern or picture.

Much of our environment is made up of repeated shapes — houses, chimneys, windows, lamp posts etc., and these form raw material for pattern pictures made with card.

A good discussion point on *similar* and *different* and so on arises.

The repetitions are linked with the rubbings on page 40. Many variations are possible by re-positioning the shapes and overlaying them.

If a shape is being printed several times, it can be more easily handled if it is glued to a piece of wood or cotton reel. Children can hold the shape much more readily *and it reduces the risk of mess.*

You will probably not want to do this very frequently but it is a simple method.

Any lump of plasticine rolled into a ball, pressed *flat* on the table and then textured by pressing into the surface ends of screws, nuts and bolts, pencils and so on will form the printing base which can be coated with colour. The plasticine is easily rolled up at any time in order to make a fresh start.

Clay will soon dry enough to be coated with colour. After a time, it will become very brittle and easily broken. Rolled out clay can give opportunities for other activities. See book 3 — "Modelling, Building and Carving".

A small lump of clay or plasticine can be used as a stamp, like a potato.

3. *Printing from Plasticine and Clay*

One of these pictures was printed on plasticine and the other on clay. If you want to make prints in this way this is how to begin:

You will need:

Some clay or plasticine.

Two strips of wood about $\frac{1}{4}$ inch thick.

A kitchen roller or roll of cardboard.

Paint and brush or rubber roller.

Newspaper and thin paper to print on. Thin kitchen paper will do, but typing paper or tissue paper is good.

Things to make marks in the clay or plasticine. Nuts, bolts, a ruler, string . . . there are many things you can think of yourself.

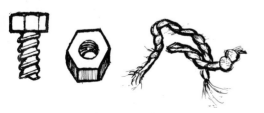

Put some newspaper on the desk and a piece of clay or plasticine on top. Put one piece of the wood on each side. How far apart are your pieces of wood? Keep them only five or six inches apart. Now roll the clay or plasticine.

You can pat it with your hand to flatten it a little first. Keep the roller on the two pieces of wood as though you were rolling along two railway lines. The picture shows you how. Soon, you will not be able to roll the clay or plasticine any thinner. Why is this?

If you wish, you can cut off the edges of the clay or plasticine to make them straight. Now make some marks in the surface. Press several of the things you have chosen into the surface. I hope you are thinking about what you are doing. Which things will make the most interesting marks? Will the pattern be better if you decide where the different things are going instead of making the marks without thinking?

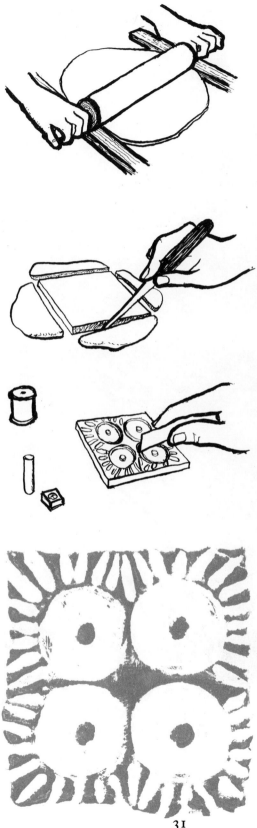

When you have made an interesting pattern in the surface, brush or roll on some thick paint or ink. Then put your paper on top and rub *lightly*. Why do you rub *lightly*?

When you have lifted off the paper, you should have a print. And you can print the same pattern again. If your print is disappointing, ask your teacher about it. I am sure that you can make some good prints this way. Try to make some better ones!

Can you find out what "corrugated" means? Do you know what this sort of card is used for? Do you think it would protect something wrapped in it? Corrugated card is used a lot and shopkeepers often have some to give away. Perhaps your teacher has some already!
You can use it for printing.

You will need:
    Corrugated card.
    A cutting knife.
    A brush or roller.
    Paint or ink.
    Thin paper.

Cut out a small piece of card. A piece about 4 inches long and 3 inches wide is big enough to start with.
Now use the knife to cut away some of the ribs of card – only the ribs. Don't go too deep.
Put the cardboard on the desk. See that it is flat.

There are various kinds of corrugated card. Some are in the form of a sandwich with a thin card on both sides and others have one ridged side. Different effects can be obtained by cutting through a varying number of layers.

Do not be dismayed by disappointing results at first. This material is worth persevering with. After all, it is an activity which is probably quite new to the children.

A useful reference book: "PRINTMAKING WITH A SPOON" by *Gorbaty*. Published by REINHOLD PUBLISHING CORPORATION.

You will realise that some of the effects obtained are capable of development when skill has increased. For young children the scope is limited, yet leaves enough for good and interesting — very often lively — results to come. One way of starting might be to print the corrugations before they are cut so that the children can, as they cut and print, compare the changes and so see what effect their cutting is having.

Cover the card with colour using a brush or roller.

Press a piece of the thin paper on to the card.

You can rub with the back of a spoon or clean roller – you may get a better print.

Carefully pull off the paper.

What has happened? Try again to see if you can do better.

Notice what has happened where you cut away the loops of the card. Now take a bigger piece of the card and see whether you can do better with a second try.

This picture was made by cutting some parts deeper than the rest. Which parts are they? See if you can make a print when you have cut the card deeper in some places.

When you have tried, discuss your work with your teacher. If you think about what you have done and then try again, you will get better prints.

5. *Printing with a Tin Can*

Have you a tin can with a lid? A syrup tin is good, but there are plenty of other tins too. Put a mark in the middle of the bottom and the middle of the lid. Make holes where you have put the marks. A good way is to put the can on a piece of wood. Then you can use a big nail and a hammer to make the holes.

Put a piece of straight wire or an old knitting needle through the hole in the bottom of the tin. Then put the wire or needle through the hole in the lid. Push the lid on to the tin. The pictures show you if you are not sure how to do it.

If you hold the ends of the wire or needle you can use the tin like a roller.
Cut some shapes of thick fabric (like felt) or rubber from an old inner tube (one from a motor tyre is good). Glue the shapes on to the tin.

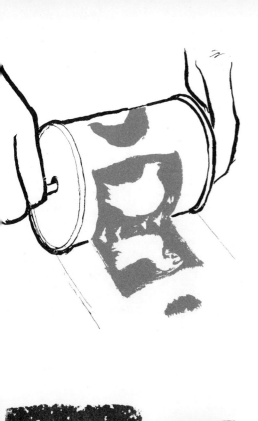

When the glue is dry, put some colour on the shapes.

An easy way to do this is to roll it over a sheet of glass or metal covered with colour or ink. You read about this on page 42.

If you have no sheet of glass or metal, you can put the colour on with a brush.

Now put a piece of paper on the desk. Run the inked or coloured roller over it. What is happening? Try again after you have put more colour on the shapes on the tin.

If you have a fresh piece of paper can you cover it with a pattern? Does it look better if you print another colour over the first?

6. *Making Rubbings*

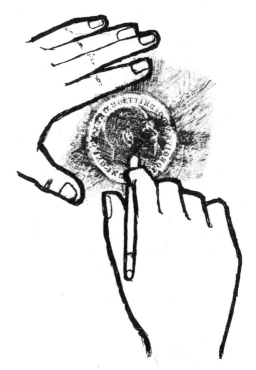

You will need :

Some thin paper (typing paper is good).

A crayon or soft pencil.

Have you a penny? Perhaps you have a coin worth more! Perhaps your teacher will lend you one.

Put the coin on the desk. Cover it with a piece of thin paper. Hold the paper with one hand so that it does not move. Rub the crayon or pencil over the paper where it covers the coin. Do not hurry! What happens?

Rubbings

Thin paper and *soft* colour are essential. Kitchen paper, typing paper, thin greaseproof paper etc. can be used and soft crayon or soft pencil will produce good results.

Tell the children how important it is to hold the paper still.

A great many textures and patterns can be obtained by rubbing and would make a very useful collection. Children, in this way, can be shown how textures and surfaces vary. The points are brought home to them more effectively than by merely feeling the surfaces. Comparisons can be made, not only between different objects but between different types or groups — wood grains, barks, leaves, stones and "mechanical" surfaces such as tyres, textiles and so on.

In addition to their attractiveness in their own right and their obvious "teaching" attributes, rubbings can often be the source of inspiration for painting and pattern work either on paper or on fabric. Why not encourage their use? Some classes make collections of rubbings and then cut them up to make collage or mosaic pictures.

An alternative method of rubbing which children find fascinating, is to rub with a candle or white wax crayon. The paper is then covered with a wash of water- or powder-colour and the rubbing will appear as if by magic. Reduce the strength of the colour by adding water and not by using white. White adds to the opacity of the colour and in some circumstances could smother the grease.

A further alternative is to use dark paper and rub with white or yellow crayon.

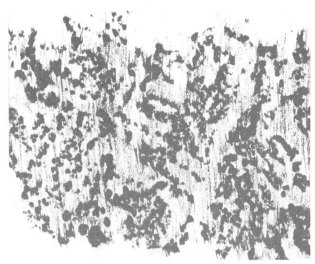

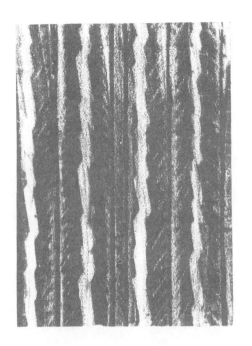

Now you can see how to make a rubbing.

Try rubbing a piece of stone. Next, try a piece of wood that is not too smooth (a railing perhaps). Is the rubbing different on wood? How is it different? What are the marks on the wood called?

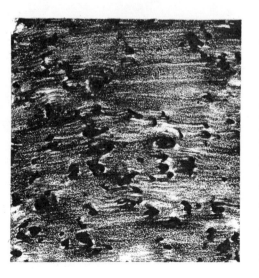

Make rubbings on the bark of trees. Do different trees give different rubbings? How many different trees can you find to rub? Have you found the names of the trees? What other things are you going to make rubbings of?

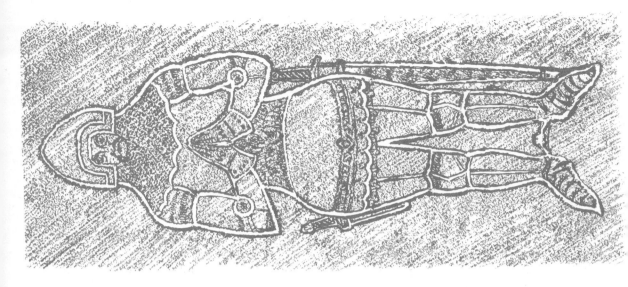

The picture shows a *brass* rubbing.
What is the man in it? How is he
dressed?
Where do you think this rubbing
was done?
Ask your teacher about brasses and
brass rubbings.
Do you know what *brass* is?

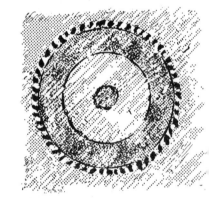

THIS STONE W

You can make a lot of different
rubbings. Why not stick them in a
book? You will soon have a collection to look at and to show.

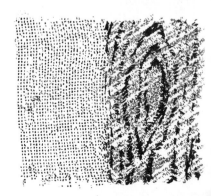

Church brasses have a great attraction for many people and their illustration of costume etc. can be useful teaching aids. If you are fortunate enough to have local brasses, please remember that some brasses have been so frequently used by rubbers that the churches concerned have had to control the activity in order to protect their treasures.

There are a number of books which provide illustrations if the real thing is not available to you.

A simple concertina book is shown, but the idea is full of possible variations.

The paper shapes will produce much better rubbings if you ensure that the children use *thick* paper from which to cut them. We suggest thick drawing paper or wrapping paper. There are more alternatives — thick sugar paper, old greeting cards etc.

You can make rubbings from paper and cardboard. Here are some rubbings made in this way.

You will need :

    A small piece of card. An old postcard will do.

    Drawing paper – the thickest you have, or wrapping paper.

    Thin paper – typing paper is good. Scissors. Paste. A crayon or soft pencil.

Cut some shapes and stick them to the card. The shapes can be just shapes or, if you want, they can be animals or people or whatever you choose. Draw them on your paper first and cut them out with scissors.

Put thin paper over the shapes and rub the crayon or the soft pencil on the paper. Have your shapes appeared? Can you do better with more tries?

The buses in the picture were printed like this. In the picture, can you see what is written on the side of the buses? The word was written on the paper shape with a hard pencil. A ballpoint pen would do it, too.

When you rub, the word comes on to the thin paper.

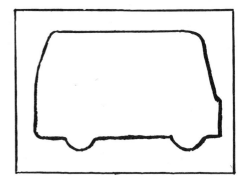

This is another way of printing using drawings on cards.

You will need :

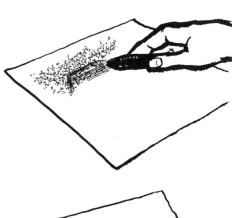

Some soft card. Any card into which you can press a mark easily with a pencil or ballpoint pen will do.

A hard pencil or a ballpoint pen. Thin paper – typing paper is good. A soft crayon or pencil.

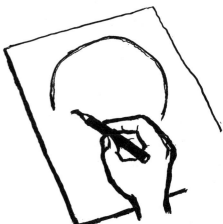

These methods of print-making have their limitations but they are a useful variant. They can be used where only a few copies of a small invitation card or greeting card are required.

Note that this method reproduces the original, not as a reflected or turned-round image, but with the shapes facing the same way.

The lettering, of course, is a refinement and can be omitted. By using coloured crayon or coloured pencil, variety is readily obtained.

It is essential to press *hard* into the card with the pencil or other instrument when drawing or writing. Make sure that the card is soft enough. You will find that most kinds of card will do, but watch out for glossy surfaces and highly-pressed cards if you are relying on card given by shops. Cardboard boxes yield a lot of material for this, and other uses.

There is enough waste material thrown out from shops and stores every week in most towns to keep several schools supplied with very useful — not to mention cheap — items.

With the pencil or ballpoint pen, draw a picture or a pattern on the card. PRESS HARD, REALLY HARD. When you have finished, put the thin paper over the card. Do not move the paper! Hold the paper and rub the crayon or pencil over it. What is happening?

Finish rubbing the paper. Make sure that you have covered all the drawing you have done.

Here is a picture done in this way. Can you do a better one? Try again.

7. *Printing Monotypes*

The picture shows a train which runs on *one* rail. It is called a *mono-rail*. *Mono* means one. Now we can read about a way of printing which many artists use. Usually, only *one* print can be made from each drawing, so it is called a *monoprint* or a *mono-type*. This sort of printing can be done on a sheet of glass, metal or formica.

You will need :

A sheet of metal (zinc is good), or some thick glass. A piece about 7 inches by 9 inches is big enough to start with.

Thin paper, a little bigger than the metal or glass.

Powder paint.

Monotypes

These are used very little in primary schools but can give very interesting results even when the more limited materials are employed.

If metal (zinc is good) or Formica (or similar) sheets are used, then not only are they safe in use but they will last many years and become almost permanent stock. The size is left to choice, we merely suggest useful dimensions. Even large books can be provided with most attractive covers by using larger sheets of metal or other alternatives. The monotype can be excellent decorative material in its own right and well worth mounting. Many artists have produced monotypes of high merit.

Ensure that any sharp edges on the Formica etc. are taped to avoid cuts.

Naturally, you will be guided by the availability of materials and whether you think it a worthwhile activity, but, like so many other things, perseverence with a new idea and its variations can bring great rewards.

Best results are obtained by using lino inks or printers' inks (cf. page 49). Printers' inks are fine, but they have the disadvantage of needing white spirit or "turps" to clean up with and they can be a nuisance if children get them on their clothes. *A water-based lino ink* is the answer. This works very well *and can be cleaned off with water.*

These inks, in a good colour range, are sold by most art suppliers. Margros and Reeves sell them in large plastic tubes which save you money. (Margros Ltd., Woking, Surrey, supply 1 lb tubes at a very reasonable price.)

Vaseline Mixture

"Vaseline" is a proprietary or trade name and you can save money by buying *petroleum jelly* in good-sized tins from chemists. If you have a commercial chemists near you, then try them first.

Mix the colour and the jelly thoroughly. You will soon find the best thickness of the rolled-out mixture to suit various purposes. Slightly absorbent paper such as "tempera" or un-glazed paper will give you good results.

Encourage the use of *bold* marks, as the pressure applied to the paper when the print is being taken will tend to push the colour inwards and so reduce the width of the marks.

This ink mixture is excellent for printing card and other shapes (cf. page 20). If you act on our suggestion of using paper which is somewhat absorbent, you will find that the mixture dries more quickly.

The area of coloured mixture can be made regular, or re-duced in size, by masking with strips of paper. An irregular shape of colour is therefore no real problem.

Vaseline (your teacher may have
a tin with petroleum jelly in it).
Rubber roller. (You can try the
cardboard roller from a toilet
roll instead. Put a brush through
the centre – picture shows you
how.)

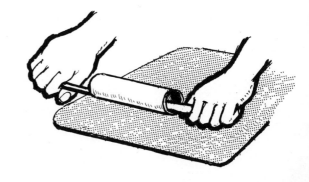

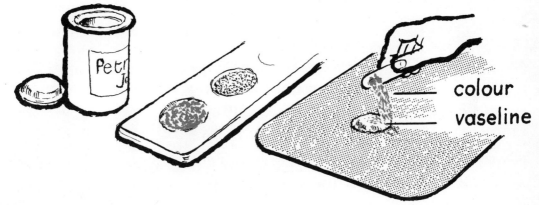

colour
vaseline

You have to mix the vaseline with
some colour.
Put a blob of vaseline on the glass or
metal. Add some colour. Roll the
vaseline and the colour together.
See that they are really mixed.

Have you a nice layer of the mixture
on the plate?
It should not be too thin. If it is,
you can add more vaseline and roll
again. If you want to make the
colour stronger, roll in some more
paint.

You will soon find out how much vaseline and how much colour you need.
Cut some paper shapes. Put them on the layer of colour and vaseline. Now press on a sheet of paper and rub hard. Do not move the paper.

If you want to see how you are getting on, you can lift up one corner of the paper. Be careful not to move the paper! Has the mixture come on to the paper? Have you got *enough* of it on the paper? If you have, pull the paper off. If you haven't, put the paper down again. Rub the paper to make more mixture come on to it. Pull the paper off.

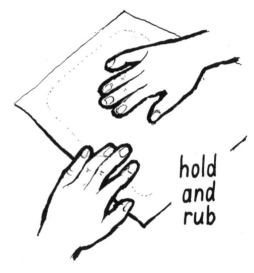

hold and rub

What has happened where you put the paper shapes?
Did you have enough vaseline and colour on the plate?
Try again and see if you can do better. Take the paper shapes off and change them if you like.

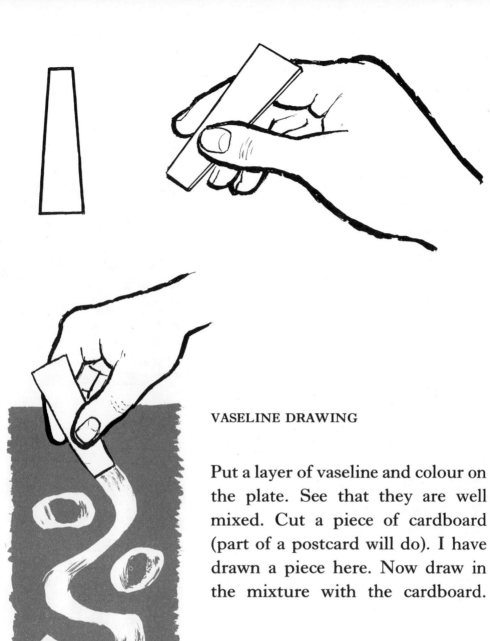

VASELINE DRAWING

Put a layer of vaseline and colour on the plate. See that they are well mixed. Cut a piece of cardboard (part of a postcard will do). I have drawn a piece here. Now draw in the mixture with the cardboard.

Press on the card and the vaseline layer will come off the glass or metal where you draw. Is the mixture sticking to your card? Wipe it off with some old paper. Go on making marks in the mixture.

Now press a piece of thin paper on to the plate. Rub hard all over the paper. Really hard!

Take a look under the paper. Lift up a corner to see. Rub again if you want to get more colour on to your paper. Take off the paper. What has happened?

The pictures show two prints made this way.

Can you do better if you try again?

Try more patterns or more pictures.

First you will have to put on more vaseline and colour and roll them out. What other things can you use to make marks in the mixture?

One idea is to use the end of a paint brush. The man on page 50 was done in this way. What are you going to try? Does it work?

MORE VASELINE DRAWING

Roll out a layer of vaseline and colour. Now place a piece of thin paper on top. *Don't press it on!*

With a pencil or ballpoint pen, draw on the paper.
Keep the paper still. The drawing shows how it is done. Draw pictures or make lines and scribbles. Try different lines – make them go in many ways. Make some thick and some thin. Make different shapes.

How many different marks can you make?

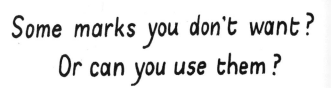

Try not to press the paper with your hands as you draw. If you do, you may make marks you don't want.

Some marks you don't want?
Or can you use them?

Lift off the paper and see what sort of printing you have done this time.

Now that you have found out how to do it, see if you can make more prints. You will need to roll on more vaseline and colour each time.

When you have finished printing, you will have to clean the glass or metal. Press old newspaper on the glass or metal and rub hard.

Do this several times. Use plenty of pieces of newspaper. This gets most of the mixture off the sheet of metal or glass. Then you can get the rest off with water and a dishcloth.

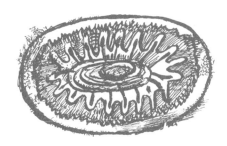

More monotypes

If you are lucky enough to have some printers' ink or lino-printing ink you can make monotypes more interesting. The inks are used instead of the vaseline and paint.

Cover the desk with newspaper and put down the sheet of metal or glass. Put some blobs of ink on the sheet. Press on a piece of thin paper. Rub it, or roll it with a *clean* roller. Pull off the paper.

Are there prints from the blobs of ink?

Now that you have seen what happens, try putting on more blobs. Make some blobs bigger than others if you want to.

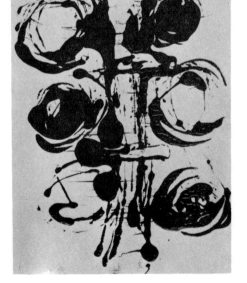

If you have other colours, see what happens when you use them.
When you have done this, and if you have enough ink, you can add more blobs or shapes and print again.

Another way of making monotypes is to roll out a layer of ink and then make patterns or pictures in it with a piece of cardboard. This is just the same as was done with vaseline on page 45.

You can print paper shapes, too. If you cannot remember how to do it, read about it again on page 44.

When you have finished printing, always clean everything ready for using later. If you have used printers' ink you will have to get it off your metal or glass sheet with turpentine or white spirit. Your teacher may have some.

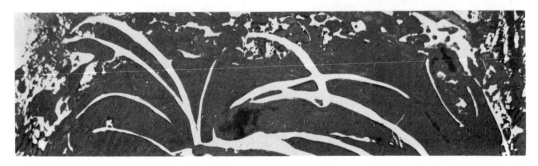

50

Printing on Fabrics

This section begins with printing methods, which have already been used and are now being applied to fabrics. These methods can be tried first with paint, in order to give the children a chance to get used to printing on fabric. This could also provide a practical demonstration of how a fast colour is needed when the fabric is washed.

Fabric inks give good results though they tend to make the material stiff. Most artists' suppliers sell them in tubes and those from:

T. N. Lawrence and Son, 2/4, Bleeding Heart Yard, Greville Street, Hatton Garden, London, E.C.I.

can be highly recommended. They have a tremendous range of colours and the fabric is not stiffened too much.

Dyes can be applied by these methods and, in the notes facing page 66, you will find information about Helizarin Dyes which are excellent in quality and very reasonable in price They are washable and light-fast and do not stiffen the material. By making a printing pad (page 14 or the alternative shown here) potatoes, string and so on can be used to give very good results on fabric.

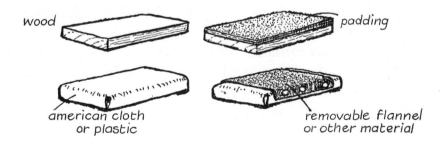

wood   padding

american cloth
or plastic

removable flannel
or other material

Printing with a screen
(The book then continues with screen printing.)
Silk screen printing is done in some schools but we are convinced that once tried, it would be very popular in many more schools. *It can be done easily and cheaply.* If you look at pages 56 and 64, you will find two very simple ideas for making a cheap, rudimentary yet effective screen. For some purposes, such as printing on paper and card, a mixture of paste and powder colour will produce good results.

If you find that screen printing is a worthwhile activity, you may like to have more permanent types of frame ready to hand. They can be made quite easily or purchased ready made from:

>   *Selectasine Ltd., 22 Bulstrode Street, London W.1 or*
>   *Dryad, Northgates, Leicester or*
>   *Ashworth Lyme Marquetry, Old Corn Mill,*
>   *New Mills, Stockport.*

To make them yourself:

1. use an old flat wooden picture frame; or

2. use four pieces of planed wood. (2 in. by 1 in. is a good size to try first.) These pieces can be fastened at the corners by L-shaped mending plates (from most do-it-yourself stores), or by nailing or screwing a short piece of wood at each corner as in the sketch.

There are other methods, but it matters little how you do it as long as one side of the frame is flat and it remains firm in use.

The material can be cotton organdie or nylon. Details of how to fasten it to the frame are mentioned on page 65 but we expand them here.

Always ensure that the material is pulled taut, without ridges, across the frame. This is easily done by starting from the middle of one side and then fastening the middle of the

8. *Printing on Fabrics*

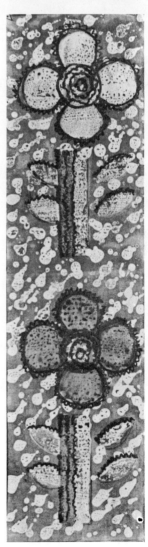

You have seen curtains and dresses and materials which have patterns printed on them. Perhaps there are some fabrics like this in the room where you are reading now. Are there? Where are they? Perhaps you are wearing something which has been printed! Is someone you can see wearing something made from a printed fabric?

Ask about printed fabrics. Find out how fabrics are made. Soon you will see how some of them are printed. *You* can print fabrics, too. Perhaps you can print some fabric and use it to make something.

I have some very nice table mats at home made by children. Some girls I know wear aprons made and printed by themselves. How pleased they were to make the whole thing themselves!

Many of the ways of printing that we have already used can also be used for printing fabrics. Can you remember some of these ways of printing? Try them on fabric.

You will need :
  Some powder paint and a brush. Some small pieces of fabric. Pieces from an old bedsheet or any cotton sheeting would be very good. Your teacher has probably got some fabric which can be used.

The fabric needs washing and ironing to make it flat for printing on. Has your fabric been washed and

opposite side. The two remaining sides are then fastened and the process continues by working outwards towards the corners (see sketches). A tacker is invaluable, but drawing pins are quite satisfactory.

A tacker is a most useful piece of equipment as it has so many uses in school, especially for setting up displays quickly. Several types are on sale, but we recommend the PRIMO tacker. Any good stationers should be able to supply you but here is the address of the firm if you need it:

The Primo Machinery Co. Ltd.,

3a, Torrens Street, London, E.C.1.

When using old nylon stocking (page 56) reject any portion containing runs or holes.

A point is made about cleaning the screen on page 63. Attention to this will cut out a number of problems later. Clean the screen before the colour has time to dry.

ironed? Put plenty of clean newspaper on the desk. Do not use paper
which has creases. Pin the material
with drawing pins to the desk or get
someone to hold the material while
you print it. Can you see why you
need paper without creases under-
neath?

Now print the material. Keep the
colour thick.

The bottom fabric on page 52 was
printed with a potato but many
other things can be used. Try some
that you have discussed with your
teacher. What would happen if you
washed the fabric you have printed?

If you are very lucky, your teacher
may have some fabric printing inks
which you can use. If so, you can
print some more fabric and you will
be able to wash it after you have
printed it.

This is how to use fabric inks:

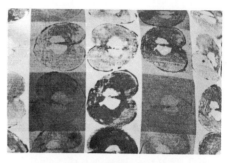

Mix some of the fabric ink with a *little* turpentine (or "white spirit") in a saucer or a tin lid. Do not make it too thin at first. You can always make it thinner when you have tried it. Use the mixture like paint – put it on with a brush or use a printing pad. (If you do not remember how to make a printing pad, look again at page 14.)

Potato, stencils, sponges . . . try all kinds of things with the ink.

The best way of all to print fabric is with a dye. Do you know what a dye is? Can you find out? Later, on

page 66, you can read how to print with dyes. But first you should know how to print with a screen.

Printing with a screen

Of all the printing methods you have used this is one of the most interesting and exciting. You can use it for fabrics and for printing on paper and card. Here are some photographs showing things printed in this way.

With a screen, you can print the same pattern or picture over and over again.

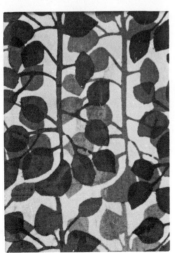

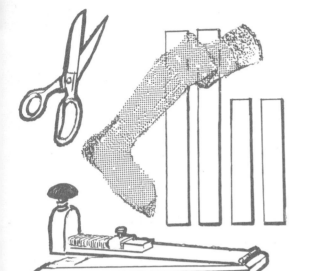

You will need :
    An old nylon stocking.
    Some strips of cardboard about
    an inch wide.
    Glue – or, better still, a stapler.
    Paper fasteners. Scissors.

Cut off a piece of the stocking near its widest end. Make sure it has no holes in it. A length of about nine inches will do. Cut down one side and open it out. Now you have to make a frame with cardboard.

Fasten four strips of card together as in the picture. Do not make it bigger than your piece of stocking.

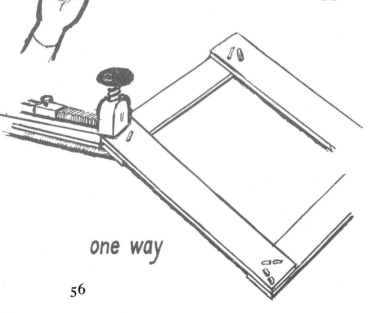

one way

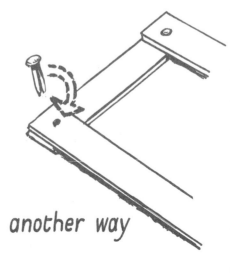

another way

About seven or eight inches long and six inches wide will do. Fasten the pieces together with paper fasteners. First, you will have to make a hole through the cardboard.

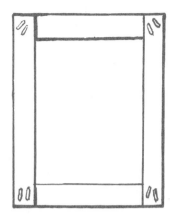

Either glue the stocking to the frame you have made or fasten it on with a stapler. Make the stocking as tight as you can. It is better when it does not sag. Cut off any pieces of stocking which are bigger than your cardboard frame.

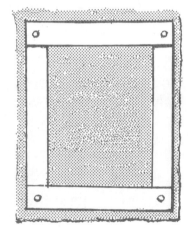

If you used a stapler, your screen is ready to use for printing. If you used glue, you will have to wait until the glue is dry.

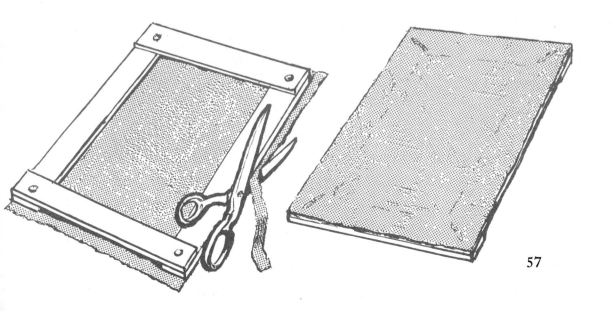

57

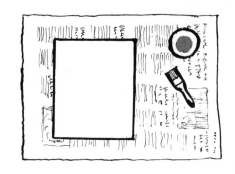

You will need :

   Paper. Paste.

   Paint (powder colour is good).

   Paste brush. Scissors.

Mix some paste (or perhaps the paste is ready for you).

Put some paint into the paste and stir well.

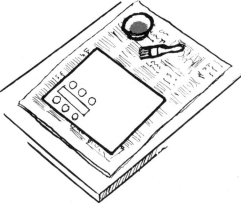

You will soon find out how much paint to put in when you start to print. If the colour is not strong enough, put more paint in the mixture.

Put some newspaper on the desk and a sheet of paper on top. Cut some shapes out of another piece of paper. Make them smaller than the screen. Any shapes will do to start with. Now put the shapes on the piece of paper. Put them where you think they will make the best pattern.

Put the screen down carefully on top of the shapes.

The work will go better if two children work together, taking it in turns; one to hold the screen still and the other to apply the colour.

Persuade them to *lift* up the screen and not to slide it when they take it off. If you wish, it can be tilted whilst one edge remains steady on the material.

Do not get the paste mixture too thin or it will run under the shapes. A sharp, clear outline will be readily obtained once the consistency of the colour is right.

A brush is suggested in the text for applying the dye, but the more usual method is to use a squeegee. The sketches show two methods of making one.

The first employs two pieces of wood fastened by nailing or, better still, screwing one on each side of a strip of rubber. Rubber merchants will sell you a small piece ¼ in. thick (or a little less would be good). The length is best determined by the inside width of the screen on which it is going to be used. The squeegee should fit nicely between the sides of the frame so that it can be pulled easily along the screen.

The second method is more of a stop-gap idea, but it works. Nail a piece of draught excluder — the rubber type with a tube running along the edge of a strip — to a batten of wood.

Pour a little of the dye into the end of the screen. Pull the dye across the screen backwards and forwards by taking the squeegee, held at an angle of about 45°, along the screen. Keep a good ridge of dye in front of the squeegee, adding more dye, in good time, at the end of the screen.

Interesting patterns can be obtained merely by turning the screen round and printing the shapes over the first print. Cleaning the screen is once again emphasised. The dye will come away easily as long as it is not allowed to dry before being cleaned with water.

The making up of the fabric after printing into all sorts of things adds to the interest aroused by the process.

Some very useful books which expand the methods mentioned here and add others:

SIMPLE SCREEN PRINTING TECHNIQUES by *Anthony Kinsey*

A pamphlet issued by the Society for Education through Art, Morley College, Westminster Bridge Road, London, S.E.1.

TEXTILE PRINTING AND DYEING by *Nora Proud*. BATSFORD

FABRIC PRINTING by *Lotti Lauterburg*. BATSFORD

If someone helps you now, you will be able to work faster and make better prints. The helper holds the screen down by pressing on the cardboard frame.

Dip your brush in the mixture of paste and colour. Brush it all over the stocking. Brush the mixture so that it goes through the stocking on to the paper. You may need to use plenty of the mixture for the first print.
Lift off the screen. Have you got a good print? Have you got too little colour on the paper or too much?

Try again. See if you can do better. Do not hurry.
The helper must press down on the frame to keep it flat and still.
Take it in turns to hold the screen while the other prints.
What colour are the shapes you have printed?
What would you do to get *coloured* shapes? Are you going to try?

Where are your paper shapes? Are they stuck to the screen? They probably are. If not, put them on the screen. The paste in the mixture will hold them.

The card in the picture has some candles on it. They were cut from paper. We printed a lot of these to send to friends at Christmas.

The second picture shows a book with a printed cover. It was made by four children who use it for their work. What has it got on it? What is the word on it?

Remember to have plenty of padding on the table or desk. A good thick wad of newsprint — say a dozen sheets — is good.

Encourage the children, as a routine, to watch the shapes as they lift the screen. Any which have not stuck to the screen — they are usually still adhering to the paper or card — can be taken off and pressed on to the screen. The paste mixture will hold them readily.

The examples give merely some ideas on using printing in a practical way. They can be added to and are by no means exhaustive.

If more than one colour is to be used on the same print, it is generally best to print the light colours first.

The attraction of cut-out letters is that they can be assembled as words or phrases in their normal order. They do not have to be reversed in order to get them to print correctly. This, of course, is a great advantage for the children.

You will appreciate that posters etc. can be readily produced by this method.

This is how to print words with a screen:

Decide how big your card is to be. How wide is it? Your word will have to be shorter than this. What would happen if it was longer?

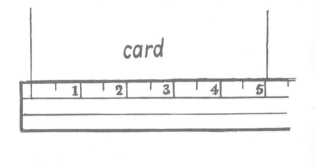

card

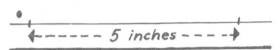

Measure this length on a piece of paper. Draw two lines or use paper with lines on it. The lines will help you to keep the letters the same size.

5 inches

The drawings show you two ways of doing the letters. Make yours as good as you can. Can you read the word easily?

Cut out each letter with scissors. Cut each one very carefully! A lot of people may want to look at your work.

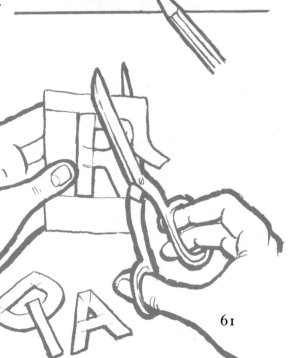

61

Draw a line on a piece of paper or card. Put the letters on this line.

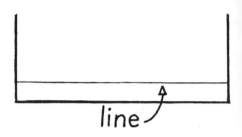

Make sure the word is not too long to go on the card you are printing. Put your screen down on top of the letters. Be careful! Look what happened to the word in the picture!

The screen was not put down in the right place! You can do better than that, can't you? See if you can.

Brush on the paste with the colour in it. Lift the screen off carefully. Make sure that the letters are stuck to the screen. If some are not, put them on the screen.

Now you can go on and print more.

Two ways of doing the letters are shown but you may very well develop ideas of your own — cutting letters from newspaper headings, for example.

If the pupils wish to do more than one word or line, it would be as well to have them space from the middle. For example:

They find the centre of the line and, having marked this, arrange the letters on either side.

Making the letters very big does not necessarily make for legibility. Letters should not be crowded together and an adequate space between each word should be allowed. Encourage the leaving of adequate margins at the sides of the paper or card.

See that the screen is not swamped with water. By holding the screen up to the light, it will be soon seen where the colour is still filling the mesh and where more gentle rubbing is needed.

A wet cloth or rag is mentioned. Other useful materials include a sponge which, if available, may be more easily and effectively used by children.

CLEANING YOUR SCREEN

You must always clean your screen well before changing the colour and, of course, you should always put your screen away clean, so it is ready for use again later. What will happen if the coloured paste is left to dry on the screen?

It is very easy to clean it. Wipe it carefully with a wet cloth or rag. Do not use too much water. Get all the paste out of the stocking. It will come out if you rub carefully. You can try rubbing with a nail brush if you have one. But be gentle! If you take care of your screen, it will last a long time.

What other ways can you think of for using the screen? The picture here shows a pattern. It was printed with a screen and then more marks were added. Look how neat it is!

Cut paper shapes and print them over and over again on a piece of paper. Why not use the paper to cover a book? What other things could you use it for? Could you print other shapes on top?

63

Another
easy-to-make screen

This is another way to make a screen. It can be bigger than the other one.

draw line

You will need :
    A cardboard box lid.
    Glue or a Stapler.
    A piece of Organdie.

Draw a line all round the lid. Draw it about one inch from the edge. The picture shows the line. Make a hole near the line and then use scissors. Cut along the line. Cut with care to make the hole tidy.

Cut the organdie about an inch bigger all round than the lid. The picture shows you what to do.
Lay the organdie flat on the desk. Put the lid down on the organdie.

The lid should be in the middle so that there is the same amount of organdie all round it.

Have you got the lid the right way up? The edges need to be upwards and the flat side against the organdie.

64

Look at the picture. Now fasten the organdie to the lid. Fasten one side first. Use glue or a stapler. Pull the organdie tight. Fasten the opposite side. Now do the other two sides.

Cut off any organdie which sticks up above the lid. If you have used a stapler, your screen is ready to use. If you have used glue, let it dry first.

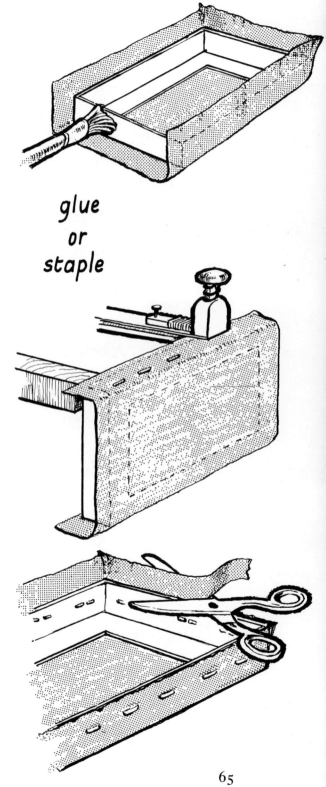

glue
or
staple

This screen is very like the ones used to print the fabrics we can buy in the shops. The curtains in my sitting-room were printed in this way. But they were not printed with coloured paste! If they were, what would happen when they were washed?

Just think what your mother would say when she washed curtains printed with paste and colour!

The fabrics we buy are printed with *dyes*. Do you know what dyes are? Can you find out about them?

Printing with dyes

Before you print a large piece of
fabric you should practise on small
pieces. Then you will know how
not to spoil the big piece.
Perhaps you have already printed
some small pieces.

You will need :
   A screen.
   A piece of fabric.
   Some dye. A brush.
   Paper shapes. Drawing pins.
Cover a desk or table with news-
paper. Stretch the fabric on top of
the newspaper. Pin it down at the
edges with drawing pins.

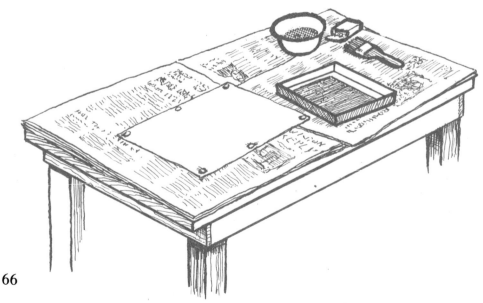

Printing with dyes

This need not be a very expensive process.

Almost any material can be used to print on as long as it is not too heavily textured. Indeed, textured materials often provide most attractive results.

Children could bring old items such as shirts and sheets. These yield good pieces of material. Make sure that the material is ironed before use in order to get it flat.

The material need not be pinned down as is suggested. It can be held down by blobs of cold water paste.

There are a number of good dyes on the market, for example: *Procion Dyes*; details from Mayborn Products Ltd.,

139/147, Sydenham Road, London, S.E.26.

and *Helizarin Dyes*: from Skilbeck Brothers Ltd.,

55/57, Glengall Road, London, S.E.15.

Both are recommended, but we have a particular liking for the Helizarin dyes as they give, perhaps, the richest colour. Both are, however, easily used and are fast to light and washing.

We give some details here of Helizarin:

Supplied in the form of paste in pots at about 3/- per oz. A suggested colour range to try: Helizarin Red T (Vermilion), Yellow G (Lemon), Blue B (Cobalt), Blue G (Prussian) and Black T. You will also need Binder D, Reduction Binder and Condensol A.

Dissolve a piece of Condensol A, sultana size, in 2 drops of water. Add 4 teaspoons of Binder D and $\frac{1}{4}$ teaspoon of dye. This will give a full strength dye. To weaken, put reduction binder in a container (a basin for example) and add dye mixture. The colours can be mixed.

To fix: allow material to dry then iron *both sides* of the material with a hot iron. Finally wash in very hot soapy water. The colours should then be fast to light and washing.

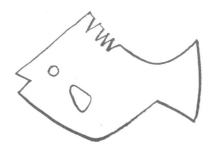

Have you cut your shapes of paper to make the pattern? Decide where you are going to put them on the fabric. Place them carefully on the fabric. Put the screen down on top of them. Get a helper to hold the screen for you. It must not move while you are printing.

Brush on the dye. Make sure it goes through the screen. First, it may be better to put the shapes on a piece of paper and print on the paper. In this way, you can be sure that the colour has started to go through the organdie. Then start to print the fabric.

When you have made the first print on the fabric, lift the screen carefully. Do not pull it along the fabric. Can you say why? Make sure that the shapes are sticking to the screen.

Go on printing until you have covered the fabric. Discuss with your teacher where you are going to put the prints before you start.

What sort of dye are you using? Your teacher will have told you. If it is a dye called HELIZARIN you must hang the fabric up to dry. When it is dry, iron it. Or get someone to iron it for you. Iron *both* sides.

When it is ironed, the fabric needs washing. Wash it twice. Let it dry. When it has been ironed again, your fabric is finished. It can be washed and the colour will stay on it. It is like the fabric you can buy in shops.

Discuss with your teacher what you can make from your fabric. What do you think you can make?
There are some pictures of printed fabrics opposite and on page 51.

Have you cleaned the screen ready for next time?

?!

Now that you have learned how to print all these things, we hope you are going to do a lot of printing. There are so many things you can make and print. Make a list of what you have done. What about making a book with prints in it?

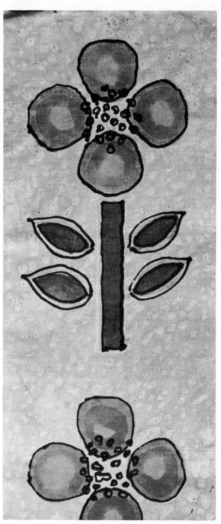

9. Tying and Dyeing

Here is a very easy way to put patterns on fabrics. You can work together with other children or do most of it yourself.

You will need:

 Small pieces of fabric.

 Some string and cotton thread.

 Cold water dye.

Try some or all of these different ways:

1.

Fold or roll your piece of fabric. The picture shows you how. Tie a knot in it. It is now ready for dyeing. Your teacher will help you with this. Put your fabric in the dye. After it has been in the dye about ten minutes, it will have to dry.

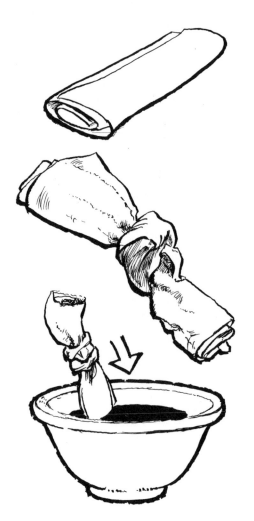

Tying and Dyeing

Such a simple method of producing interesting patterns on fabric deserves to be much more widely appreciated.

Varied results can come from the use of different tying materials. Do see that more than one is available. String will give results which differ from those using cotton thread. But string can be obtained in various sizes and types. For example, there is thin, "hard" string and the thicker, softer types. Let the children try them all.

Have the children tie their thread or other tying material as tightly as they can and do see that the knots are firm!

Many other ways of handling the fabric can be employed. Stitching gives interesting results. There are books (see previous notes and later), which go more thoroughly into the subject than is possible here. Do not be afraid, however, of trying out, or letting the children try out, variants and new methods. "What happens if we do this?" is the attitude we want.

Any dye into which the tied or stitched fabric can be placed will do. Dylon or Drummer are good examples and *Skilbeck Bros. Ltd, 55/57 Glengall Road, London, S.E.15* supply *SOLAMINE* dyes in tins.

The dye can be mixed in a pan, though some schools prefer an old zinc bath.

Allow the material time to take up the dye and then ensure that it is dry before untying it.

Interesting results accrue if several dippings in different colours are made. For example, a white material tied and dyed yellow, when tied again and dyed blue, will give a pattern of yellow, blue and green. If you wish, some or all of the first tying can be left when the second is done. The original colour of the material will be left when the operation is completed, in addition to the dyed colours.

Encourage a variety of attempts at any one treatment.

Different sorts of tying can be done on one piece of material and, of course, the amount of material actually tied can be varied.

Once again, the whole process takes on greater significance when things which can be used by the children are produced from the patterned material.

Some teachers encourage their children to add stitching to the tie and dye pattern and other forms of printing can be added as an alternative, or an addition.

What can you get the children to suggest? Aprons, curtains, scarves, headsquares . . . ?

Books:

TEXTILE PRINTING AND DYEING by *Nora Proud*. BATSFORD.
TIE AND DYE AS A PRESENT DAY CRAFT by *Anne Maile*. MILLS AND BOON.

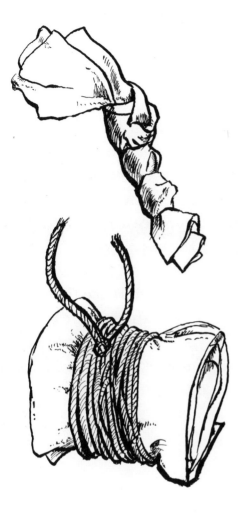

When it is dry, undo the knot. What has happened? Why is there a shape on your piece of fabric?

If you wish, you can tie the fabric again and put it in a dye of a different colour. What happens this time? Is the result better?

Of course, you can tie more than one knot in your fabric and see if you like the result. Try using two dyes. With the first, tie the fabric once. With the second, tie it twice.

Do you like *that* way of doing it?

2.

Roll the fabric together tightly into a small bundle. Tie it with string or cotton. Put it in the dye. Dry it. What is the fabric like when you have cut the string or cotton? Tie other pieces in different ways. Is there a difference when you use string instead of cotton, or cotton instead of string?

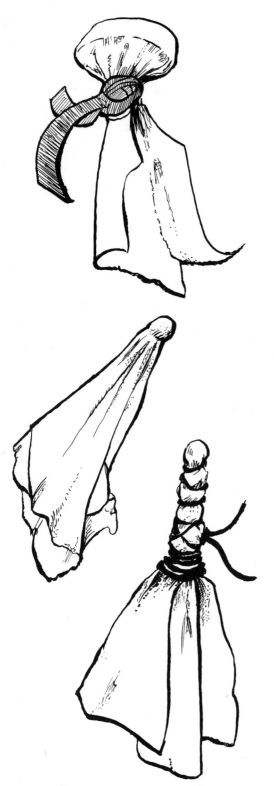

3.

Put a pebble or a coin or a plastic bottle-top in the fabric. Tie it in. Try tying it with tape, or wool or something else you can think of. What have you got which you can use? Put it in the dye. Does it make any difference to the result?

Can you use this difference to make different marks on the fabric? What happens if you tie some parts with one thing and other parts with something different?

4.

Pull the fabric from the middle with your thumb and finger. Make it hang down. A pin or a bead can help you if you put it in the fabric first. The picture shows how the fabric is pulled together. Tie it tightly with string or cotton or whatever you want to try. Dye the fabric. Is this different from the other results?

Now try a piece of fabric tied in more than one place. Like the one in the picture here. It does look rather funny, doesn't it? But when it is dyed and opened out again it will look very different. Do you like the result?

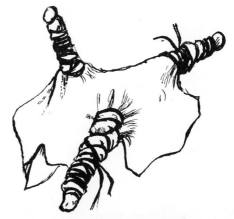

All these pieces of fabric can have other prints put on top of the marks you have made. Here are some done in this way. This is called OVER-PRINTING.

The pattern on the apron in the picture has been over-printed. You can over-print. Try it and see if you like the fabric better.

Can you make your printed fabric into something useful?
The pictures give you some ideas. I am sure you can think of others. Talk about your ideas with your teacher.
The apron in the picture has had some braid and stitches added.
The girl who made it was very pleased with it.
Do you like it?

It is essential to get the children to put plenty of wax into the material.

A more effective way of putting on the wax, if you have the facilities, and can control it, is to warm the candle or paraffin wax until it melts. Use an old pan and *do not overheat. It could be dangerous.* An open flame would be more dangerous than, say, an electric heater. But the method is an exciting one and is worth the care exercised.

Take the pan to the fabric so that the wax does not harden on the brush before it is applied to the material.

This is called a *resist* method and is used frequently in decoration, especially in pottery.

If the dye is brushed on, you can apply several colours if you wish.

Printing and dyeing using wax

In another book, you can read about making patterns on paper with a candle and paint. Here is how to do it on fabric.

You will need :
   A piece of fabric.
   Cold water dye or Helizarin dye.
   A candle.
Put some newspaper on your desk and pin down the fabric on top with drawing pins. If you cannot pin your fabric, work with a helper who can hold the edges of the fabric. Draw shapes and lines on the fabric with the candle. Press the candle *really hard* on to the fabric so that you put on plenty of candle grease.

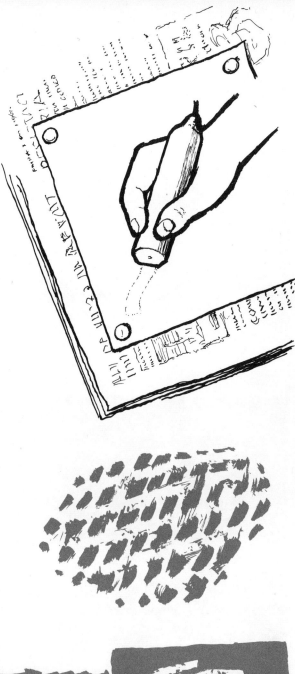

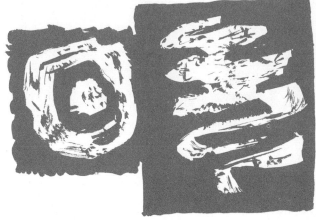

Here are two different ways of adding the colour.

1. Put the fabric into a cold water dye. This is the dye used for the tie and dye printing on page

2. Paint the fabric all over with Helizarin dye – if you have some. Let it dry. Iron it or get someone to iron it for you.

To take off the wax in both cases, put the fabric on to newspaper.

Cover it with blotting paper and iron it. The warm iron will melt the wax. The wax will run into the blotting paper and make the fabric softer.

See what you can find out about printing with wax. Many fabrics are printed with wax. Can you find out which they are and which countries they come from?

Paste

This is another resist method. Results are different from those obtained by the wax method, as the paste gives much less resistance. Charming results, however, are readily obtained. Resist patterns can be built up on paper — see *Book 5*, *Picture and Pattern Making*.

Try different thicknesses of paste to test the results and remember, once again, that this method can be used in combination with other forms of printing and dyeing.

10. *Paste Patterns*

You can use *paste* to make patterns on fabric.

Mix some paste – flour and water will do – and put it on your fabric *thickly* to make the pattern. A very good way to put the paste on is to put it in a plastic bottle. You need one with a small cap which you can take off to put the paste in. A washing-up liquid bottle is good.

Squeeze the paste on to the fabric making dots and lines and shapes.

Let it dry. Then put the dye on with a roller. When the fabric is washed your pattern will show like the ones in the pictures.

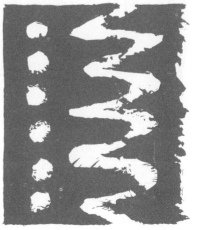

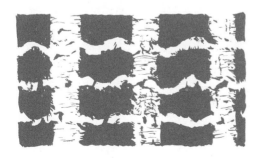

I hope you have enjoyed doing different kinds of printing. If you do things several times you should get better and better prints and patterns.

Do some of the printing again. First, think about what you are going to do. Think about the shapes you cut.

Think about where you are going to put them. Think about different ways of using some of the things you have read about or others you have thought of yourself.

Talk about your ideas with your teacher and friends. Discuss what

It cannot be over-emphasised that, although a lot of information is given in this book, you and your children will gain immensely by looking into variations of the methods mentioned.

Some suggestions have been made in these teacher's notes about some of the possible variants but there are many more possibilities if you can develop an attitude of probing and of experiment. As we said in the introduction, many types of development are possible. Remember to use every means you can of raising interest and enthusiasm. Materials, "found objects", pictures, natural objects, magazines, books, visits, all play their part. Discussion with the children is vital and can improve their work immensely.

The book has been written to help and *not to restrict*. There should be no suppression of a child's experimental method just because it does not correspond to the instructions in this book. If no serious disaster or undue frustration is imminent, allow the child to try his own way.

The book should be a big help but it cannot replace you, the teacher. Given your interest, given your encouragement — especially to find out and explore — a child should be able to obtain a large amount of satisfaction and plenty of enjoyment by using the book.

Do not be afraid to try; do not be afraid to make mistakes.

SUPPLEMENTARY MATERIALS

Suppliers of materials mentioned in this book:
Printing Frames
Ashworth Lyme Marquetry, Old Corn Mill, New Mills, Stockport.
Dryad Ltd., Northgates, Leicester (who also supply most other materials).
Selectacine Ltd., 22 Bulstrode St., London W.1.
Inks and dyes
T. N. Lawrence & Son, 2 Bleeding Heart Yard, Greville St., London E.C.1.
Mayborn Products Ltd., 139/147 Sydenham Rd., London S.E.26. (Procion dyes).
Skilbeck Bros. Ltd., 55/7 Glengall Rd., London S.E.15. (Helizarin dyes.)
Water based printing dyes
Margros Ltd., Woking, Surrey.
Reeves & Sons Ltd., Lincoln Rd., Enfield, Middx.
Staple gun
Primo Machinery Co. Ltd., 3a Torrens St., London E.C.1.

Books
Creative Print Making, Peter Green. Batsford.
Fabric Printing, Lotti Lauterburg. Batsford.
Print Making with a Spoon, N. Gorbatry. Reinhold Printing Corporation.
Textile Printing and Dyeing, Nora Proud. Batsford.
Tie and Dye as a Present Day Craft, Anne Maile. Mills and Boon.

Pamphlet
Simple Screen Printing Techniques, Anthony Kinsey, from the Society for Education through Art, Morley College, Westminster Bridge Road, London, S.E.1.

you have done and what you could do to make your printing better.

Don't be afraid to try. Don't be afraid to make mistakes. Say to yourself: "I'm going to see what happens if I do it in a different way" or "I'll print in one way and then print in another way on the same piece of paper."

If you keep on trying and thinking you will enjoy your printing more and get some very interesting prints to look at and to show.
Good luck!

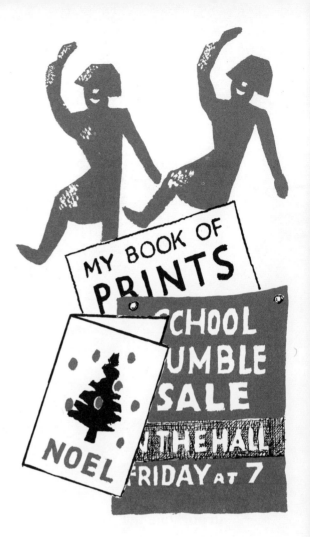

Index